The Ballygally Book

An Autobiography of

Michael Sheane

A.H. STOCKWELL
PUBLISHERS SINCE 1898

Published in 2024 by
Michael Sheane
in association with
Arthur H Stockwell Ltd
West Wing Studios
Unit 166, The Mall
Luton, Bedfordshire
ahstockwell.co.uk

To the people of Ballygally

Also from Michael Sheane

Ulster & Its Future After the Troubles (1977)
Ulster & The German Solution (1978)
Ulster & The British Connection (1979)
Ulster & The Lords of the North (1980)
Ulster & The Middle Ages (1982)
Ulster & St Patrick (1984)
The Twilight Pagans (1990)
Enemy of England (1991)
The Great Siege (2002)
Ulster in the Age of Saint Comgall of Bangor (2004)
Ulster Blood (2005)
King William's Victory (2006)
Ulster Stock (2007)
Famine in the Land of Ulster (2008)
Pre-Christian Ulster (2009)
The Glens of Antrim (2010)
Ulster Women – A Short History (2010)
The Invasion of Ulster (2010)
Ulster in the Viking Age (2011)
Ulster in the Eighteenth Century (2011)
Ulster in the History of Ireland (2012)
Rathlin Island (2013)
Saint Patrick's Missionary Journeys in Ireland (2015)
The Story of Carrickfergus (2015)
Ireland's Holy Places (2016)
The Conqueror of the North (2017)
The Story of Holywell Hospital: A Country Asylum (2018)
Patrick: A Saint for All Seasons (2019)
The Picts: The Painted People (2019)
Pictland: The Conversion to Christianity of a Pagan Race (2020)
Irish & Scottish Dalriada (2020)
The Roman Empire (2021)
The Ancient Picts of the Scottish Highlands of the Seventh Century (2021)
The Celtic Supernatural (2022)
Grace O'Malley, Pirate Sea Queen of Ireland (2023)
Ireland, 1588 (2023)

Contents

Chapter One 1

Chapter Two 5

Chapter Three 8

Chapter Four 10

Chapter Five 16

Chapter Six 18

Chapter Seven 21

Chapter Eight. 24

The Ballygally Book

Chapter One

I was born at St Neots, Huntingdonshire (now part of Cambridgeshire), England, on the 27th of June 1947 in a country that was recovering from six years of world war, and when the British Empire was still in existence. My parents, Eric and Annie Sheane, were Irish who had moved to England in 1938; my father was a dentist and mother a housewife. I do not remember much about my early years but I have vague memories of windmills on the Fens. My brother Derek was six years older than me but even though he had gone to primary school in England, he had retained an Irish accent. I had a semi-English accent, though was never taken for an Irishman. My mother said that I fancied myself as a bit of an Englishman. I was baptised in Godmanchester and I still have a copy of the birth certificate, which in later years I carried in my wallet

I was born into an England that had elected a Labour Government, the Prime Minister being Mr Clement Attlee who had been Deputy Prime Minister in Winston Churchill's National Government that saw the defeat of Adolf Hitler and the division of Germany into two states: West and East Germany. My father had gone to school in Coleraine in County Londonderry and had attended the Coleraine Academical Institution; my mother had left school early on to be brought up on a farm in County Down. In my father's day there was no such thing as academic grants or scholarships to university. When he left school he had had a variety of jobs which financed his studies at Queens University,

Belfast, to become a dentist but neither myself nor my brother Derek followed in his footsteps.

In my day television was in its infancy and there was only one channel: the BBC. But there was BBC Radio that had broadcast Winston Churchill's speeches during the war. My brother Derek had vague memories of troops moving from England into Germany during the war. By the time I developed a full memory I was living in Northern Ireland in Draperstown, a village in the Druim Dearg mountains in County Londonderry. My father and mother wanted to give me an Irish education but my mother was sad at leaving St Neots.

At Druim Dearg, my mother and father had rented a country house and my father continued his career as a school dental officer. I have memories of my brother Derek learning how to ride a bicycle.

We did not live long in Draperstown before we left to live in Riverdale Park Road, Finaghy, West Belfast, for which I have many accurate memories. Our next-door neighbour was English and the little girl I played with, Patricia Tuck, was also English. Riverdale Park Road was mainly Protestant, but there were a few Roman Catholics. Although no friend of the Orange Order, my father was a non-practising member of the Church of Ireland and he and my mother were married in the church.

I was sent to Finaghy Primary School, whose Headmaster was Mr Brown. At first my mother walked the two-mile journey with me to the school, but as I grew older I made the journey on my own. I remember the air-raid shelters at the school and alas at about five or six years of age there was the dangerous habit of smoking cigarettes. At Finaghy Primary School I took an interest in running and other sports, competing at sports day.

My father bought a television when we were at Riverdale Park Road; he watched it in his bedroom lying in bed and I would lie beside him. He also had a 9.5mm cine projector with films that featured Mickey Mouse.

When we were at Riverdale Park Road he became the Assistant County Dental Officer for Antrim. He had a black Ford Prefect and we would make trips to places in Northern Ireland including the Mourne Mountains. The car had cost the vast sum of £50.

I was learning about the Orangemen and the Protestant nature of the Northern Ireland state. My mother took me to the field where the Orangemen met each 12th of July where they celebrated the victory of King William of Orange over the Catholic English King James II – but I was not impressed with the Orange Order.

Soon my uncle Jim, a widower, said he wanted my mother to come and look after him in his old age, so in 1955 we left Finaghy for Ballygally, a seaside village on the Antrim coast, five miles from the seaport of Larne and about a forty-five-minute drive from Finaghy. My uncle lived in a seaside bungalow looking out into the bay. The cost of building the bungalow had been about £500, and it had three bedrooms, a hall, a front room looking out to the sea, a toilet, a living room which had a large fireplace, and a kitchen. Outside the bungalow there was a garage, but uncle Jim did not have a car. There was a large front and back garden. Jim Heslip was in his early eighties; he and my mother had been friends from an early age. He was a staunch Orangeman who put out a Union Jack on the 12th of July and watched the Orangemen parade through Ballygally on their way to Belfast to the field at Finaghy. My uncle Jim had retired when he was forty, having made a lot of money supplying the ships at Belfast; he had a substantial private income a result of his hard work. His account was with the Ulster Bank in Larne.

My father was not a churchgoer, but at Ballygally my mother walked up the Cairncastle Road to St Patrick's Church of Ireland, where the rector was the Reverend Brown, but who would die in 1957 at a relatively young age.

By the time we were living in Ballygally, my father was the sole County Dental Officer, based at Rostulla in Belfast.

When I was about five years of age my mother had taken me to York Road Railway Station in Belfast, where we introduced ourselves to the train driver – I wanted to be a train driver. Sometimes we had taken the train from Belfast to Larne, a journey by rail of about forty-five minutes; from Larne we caught the bus to Ballygally where the bus stop was at the end of the bungalow's drive. The train stopped at Jordanstown, Troopers Lane, Carrick Fergus, Whitehead, Ballycarry, Magheramourne, Glynn and Larne Town. I quite enjoyed travelling by train, more so than in my father's Ford Prefect. I also liked the bus journey to Ballygally, a journey of about twenty minutes on the number 162 bus that had as its destination Cushenden, up the Antrim Coast Road.

Chapter Two

I was five years of age when my parents moved into the bungalow, which was called Glyn-Ouley; in those days there were no numbers on the houses. Uncle Jim's wife had died when she was young, so Uncle Jim would be happy for the company.

It was not long before I made friends with Christopher Harbinson. I would run up the long drive to the large white house that overlooked the bay. His father was Kenneth Harbinson, a Director of Howden's Coal Company based at Larne Harbour. There were four children in the Harbinson family but their mother died when Chris was about five; he had been greatly attached to her. She would take Chris by the hand and walk him down to the bus stop outside the bungalow where he and myself and other children caught the school bus to Larne Grammar School where I started to attend at the age of five.

Larne Grammar School was situated at the end of Cairncastle Road and had in all about three hundred pupils; the primary school department had four teachers headed by Miss Neill, who encouraged me to write poetry – I had a poem, which she helped me to write, published in the school magazine.

In the dining room of the bungalow my mother cooked our meals; Cornflakes, an Ulster fry for breakfast, and tea and toast with marmalade before I left the bungalow at about 8:30 a.m. to travel to my primary school with Chris. The buses were painted green and owned by the Ulster Transport Authority, the first nationalised industry in Northern Ireland. There were single-decker buses for the arch at Drains Bay on the road to Larne that could not take double-decker buses. The fare from Ballygally to Larne was only a penny ha'penny and each bus had a conductor.

In 1955, Ballygally had a population of about three hundred, the houses being situated along the seafront and in Grace Avenue. Ballygally Hill or Head rose three hundred feet and I climbed it with Chris on many occasions. Back then, there was no golf course on the fields that swept back from the summit of Ballygally Head. There was a house in the region that was owned by Mr Elim Thompson, the editor of the *Larne Times*, read by everyone in Ballygally. Mr Thompson had a son called Johnny Thompson with whom I made friends. Originally the Harbinson's house at Ballygally had a flat roof and was painted white; later on a roof was added to the house in the 1960s. On many occasions I was invited to have a meal with the Harbinsons, whose house had a large kitchen. I ate a number of interesting meals in their large dining room.

My brother Derek also played with the other Harbinson children – John, Denny and Judith, who in later life bought a car costing five pounds. Ballygally Head was quite an historical place dating back to Stone Age times and was excavated by archaeologists. From the summit of the Head it was possible to see Scotland, and from there early man may have reached the Antrim coast in their wooden boats. Ballygally in Gaelic meant the townland of the rocks. The residents at the east side of the bay fashioned harbours out of the rocks into ports for their rowing and sailing boats. When my father built three boats he fashioned a port out of the rocks in front of the bungalow. My father had a Sabre speedboat, a GP sailing boat and a fibreglass dinghy.

On one occasion we travelled out to the Maidens Lighthouses lying five miles off the Antrim coast in the Larne region. I could not swim so my father was reluctant to let me sail by myself in the boats. There was an impressive beach at Ballygally along with two boathouses, one of which housed Larne boat club but had ceased to be used by the time we moved to Ballgally. However, Derek along with his friend Randal Orr were allowed to use the boats as they could both swim. The bay at Ballygally was used by the residents for bathing and swimming; with the advent of motor cars the population of Ballygally increased dramatically at weekends.

In the early 1960s the old stone wall on the seafront was disbanded and railings constructed, with entrances down to the beach. In 1959 there were two shops in Ballygally, a Post Office-cum-grocery store and a café, which survived until recent times. Today there is no Post Office, but a Spar shop was erected recently. Since the '60s most of the population of Ballygally have cars and shop in Larne, with the bus also being used. Ballygally, I think, is a middle-class village but has few large houses like the Harbinson's house.

When my uncle Jim died in 1957, he left a lot of money to my parents. My mother had fitted carpets laid and disposed of the ancient furniture, replacing them with modern chairs and tables; she also had the bungalow newly decorated throughout. My father bought himself a new Ford Zodiac that cost him one thousand pounds. Uncle Jim also left me thirty pounds in his will along with stocks and shares for my parents that provided an income.

Our next-door neighbour at Ballygally was a Mr Sydney Durbridge, an Englishman and a film distributor; his house was called The Bungalow but was a two-storey affair. When my brother Derek was about sixteen, he wanted to have a job and Sydney gave him employment, helping in his film distribution business. Sydney had a TR3 sports car that Derek liked to drive around Ballygally in, despite the fact that he was not yet seventeen. However, Sydney wanted to return to live in England. Now my brother joined the RAF to continue his education, but he did not take to the RAF and bought himself out to attend Larne Grammar School with a view to going to Queens University, Belfast.

Chapter Three

I was now about thirteen years of age, still at Larne Grammar School, but now in the Senior School, where I learned to play rugby. But I did not like Larne Grammar, so my father sent me to a boarding school in County Tyrone called The Royal School of Dungannon. I did not like this either. I wanted my father to send me to Orange's Academy in Belfast – a mixed Protestant and Catholic school, but mainly Catholic. My father agreed; I was now at my heart's content with this little male-dominated school that had only one hundred and fifty pupils; there was no pressure put upon me to receive the beliefs of the Church of Rome.

My father's headquarters were in Alexander Gardens, Belfast, just off the Antrim Rd. Each morning he would drive me to Belfast and at Alexander Gardens I caught the bus into central Belfast where I walked to Orange's. On days that my father was not working in Belfast, I caught the train to York Road in the city; from there I walked up York Street to Chapel Lane in which the Academy was situated overlooking the Catholic Grotto.

In the classroom I could hear the priests chanting the Hail Mary ('Ave! Ave! Ave, Maria'). The Principal of Orange's was Mr Coleman, a devout Catholic who taught mathematics, geography and French. Both Larne Grammar and Dungannon Royal were bigoted schools and from an early age I realised that Ballygally's residents were no friends of Roman Catholics. But on the other hand, I had no ambition to be received into the Catholic Church. My friends at Orange's Academy were mostly Roman Catholics.

As a teenager in Ballygally I was a bit of a mischievous fellow and two or three families were instructed not to befriend me, but the Harbinsons did not take this attitude and I was always welcomed at High Corners, the name of the Harbinsons' house.

Education at Orange's was only to 'O' Level, so I attended the Jaffa college on the Antrim Road and I managed to obtain enough grades to attend Trinity College in Dublin. At the Jaffa College I met Gillian Harvey, who I befriended; she was about nineteen and spoke with an English accent, her father being the Managing Director of Harland and Wolff. Trinity College was full of bigoted students from Northern Ireland, so after a year I left Ireland to work in London as a Staff Consultant, placing mostly women in jobs. The staff at Josephine Salmon's bureau were surprised that I was an Irishman because I spoke with an English accent. But this was not the first time I had been in London. My parents had brought me on holiday on two occasions in 1959, the first time by air from Nutts Corner in a Viscount aircraft and again that year by road and rail. London would soon come to be known as the swinging city, now that the British Empire was a thing of the past and the British Commonwealth of Nations had taken political root. I loved London and visited all the famous sights and took a number of photos. I visited the Tower of London, where so many traitors had been jailed for their beliefs, both religious and political. Perhaps it was upon my first visit to the city that I developed a love for the English, for London was not a bigoted place.

Chapter Four

My brother Derek and his wife Helen had now also left Ballygally, to work in Manchester. He worked for ICI, training managers for the corporation. He had graduated from Queen's University in psychology, a four-year course. I went north to join him in 1970, to become a self-employed printer selling personal stationery and printing to businesses. I had two printing machines, one being an Adana 8x5 and the other a Thompson 11x7 treadle platen. I sold printing for fourteen years from a two-up two-down terraced cottage in the village of Bredbury near Stockport in the Manchester area, but part of Cheshire.

My father died in December 1970; he was plagued with depression and had taken an accidental overdose of sleeping tablets and the verdict at his inquest was 'open'. He was cremated in a service held by Revd Caldwell and buried in the graveyard of Saint Patrick's Church of Ireland, overlooking Ballygally Bay. He had previously left his job as County Dental Officer for Antrim and built a large greenhouse in the back garden of the bungalow and called the business The Paradise Garden Centre, but died before he advertised the greenhouse.

I was not green-fingered so I sold the greenhouse for £100, having advertised it in the *Belfast Telegraph*. I was fan of motorbikes and sold my father's Vauxhall Viva for £600. I lived in Ballygally for three months to help my mum to get over my father's death. In March 1970, having bought a Honda 175, that I left for Manchester to continue selling printing.

My mother was left alone in Ballygally; she was sixty but still able to cut the extensive front and back lawns, which took many hours; she also cut the privet hedges that my father had planted to adorn the bungalow. There were also rose-beds that my father had made and these had to be looked after. To get herself out of the house she started to do voluntary work in Glenarm, a little townland lying about seven miles from Ballygally. When she became very old (she lived until she was eighty-seven), she employed a gardener to come in and cut the lawns and trim the privet hedges.

When I was in my teens I had always looked forward to Sundays. Not because I was a church goer, but because my mother and father took trips up the Antrim Coast Road where the Glens of Antrim terminate at Cushedall, a distance of some twenty-five miles from Ballygally. My mother would brew up a flask of tea and would have made some cheese-and-tomato sandwiches. We would stop at Carnlough to have an ice-cream; in those days the ice-cream firm was Ulster Creameries. A slider of ice-cream cost a shilling and a bottle of Coca-Cola about the same.

Ballygally Castle Hotel is a base for tourists that want to visit the Glens of Antrim. Ballygally Castle lies in the centre of the village and dates back to 1624 when it was built by James Shaw of Greenock, who also had land in County Down. This was the age of the start of the Plantation or Colonisation of Ulster, with Scots and English folk. Ballygally Castle, as castles go, is not very large and the hotel part is of modern construction. In the castle building there is a pub that sells a good Bushmills whisky, and there is believed to be a ghost at the top of the stairs. I did not frequent Ballygally Castle until I was in my forties, but I was always intrigued with this planter's bawn that had a river flowing through it that runs into the sea at Ballygally. For some years the castle was owned by the carpet magnet Cyril Lord, who renamed the castle Candlelight Inn. Cyril Lord sold Ballygally Castle to the Hastings group of companies and it was renamed Ballygally Castle Hotel and this is the situation that remains today. For some years the Shaw family owned the castle, but it was eventually taken over by hoteliers after the end of the Second World War. Ballygally Castle is modelled after a Scots baronial-style castle, with its candle-snuffer roofs. Moving along Ballygally seafront, the visitor comes to the Halfway House which is a pub that has bed-and-breakfast facilities situated at the end of Ballygally village. All along the seafront there are expensive houses and bungalows. Kenneth Harbinson's brother Gerald lived in quite a large house in a road running up to it from the coast road. As a child I used to play with Richard Harbinson and his younger brother Peter. In the early sixties this was the age when children played Cowboys and Indians; the girls played the Red Indians with their long hair and the boys, with their short back and sides, played Cowboys. My parents bought me a Cowboy suit and a little model gun; I played Cowboys and Indians mostly with Chris Harbinson while Penny and Judith played the Indians. My favourite Cowboy was The Lone Ranger which was shown at Children's Hour on the BBC, long before there was any Ulster Television in Northern Ireland. Ulster Television started to broadcast when I was at Larne Grammar.

My father also bought me to the cinema at Larne, at a time when there were queues outside for very popular films such as *The King and I*. The cinema at the end of Main Street in Larne of course showed many westerns, in the age of Cowboys and Indians. There was another cinema in Larne called the Savoy which I did not frequent, but its owner's son went to Larne Grammar, a middle-class school in the sixties. My brother Derek and his friend John Harbinson were a little too old to play Cowboys and Indians, although John had a large Colt 45 model. He and Derek made a raft cut out of barrels with a plank on top and sailed it in the bay, long before my father made the boats.

From Ballygally Bay there is a good view of the Sallagh Braes, lying on the edge of the Antrim Plateau. In winter the braes come alive with waterfalls from the heavy rain. At the foot of Ballygally Head is O'Halloran's Castle – now a ruin – which Chris and I climbed up into. In the past it was the home of a poet called Agnew. There is a legend that states that a tunnel runs from the Castle under Ballygally Bay into the headland of MacCauley.

When we had the boats, we rowed the short journey from Ballygally Bay to O'Halloran's Castle, which in early days may have been a two- or three-storey affair. There is a good view of the Castle from the top of Ballygally Head, not really a headland for it only rises three hundred feet above the sea. Again, like Ballygally Castle, O'Halloran's is not really a castle with its two or three small rooms of stone taken from the nearby beach of rocks.

I had two other friends in my teens at Ballygally: Hugh Steele and Kenny Aillen, who lived in the coastguard houses near the two shops. My parents travelled up the Coast Road, after leaving behind Glenarm and its Castle that belonged to the Earl of Antrim. We came to Carnlough with its harbour situated in the centre of the town. From here ships traded with Scotland; there was also another harbour at Glenarm which supplied Scotland with limestone quarried locally. The Earl of Antrim did not rule all of County Antrim but did live in a large mansion within its own grounds. The entrance to the house was via Castle Street in the centre of Glenarm.

I have all the scenic places of the Antrim Coast and Glens on 8mm cine film and my father took many colour photographs of this twenty-five mile stretch.

After Carnlough we would stop to take photos of Red Bay, so called because of the colour the beach. There is a ruined MacDonnell castle on a small headland overlooking Waterfoot. The MacDonnells who owned Glenarm Castle ruled the Catholics of the Antrim Glens, there being nine Glens in all. My favourite is Glendun with its large viaduct at the foot of the Glen which runs from Newtown Crommlin some twenty miles up the road, with turf to be had on the side of the road.

Before I had a cine camera, Chris and I made a hiking tour of the Antrim Hills that lay to the east of the plateau. We hiked up the Cairncastle Road to a region that had a Unitarian Church and Presbyterian Church; there was also a well. A little further to the west is Saint Patrick's Church of Ireland where both my mother and father are buried. Now we started the climb to the top of Knock Dhu Mountain at the summit of which there is a good view of Ballygally with the Harbinsons' house standing out. It also looks down to a valley full of rocks.

Onward we hiked with our tent to the region of Deer Park River where we stopped at the bridge overlooking the fast-flowing waters. We decided to camp at Deer Park but were cursed with flies, forcing us to pitch our tent elsewhere. We boiled up potatoes and corned beef along with a can of beans. By this time Chris had become a pupil of Royal School Portora, Enniskillen, where he was a boarder and I was at Orange's Academy in Belfast.

The road winds on from Deer Park to the hamlet of Aughafatten, which has a post office that serves the farming community. At length we came to Carnalbanagh, a small townland with some houses and from here we at last came to Newtown Crommelin that was situated on a slight hill. On the approach to the village there are a number of pubs. We were too young to imbibe so we had to put up with lemonade. The local newspaper covering the area was the *Ballymena Guardian,* which lay relatively close to Newtown Crommelin. From here we started the hike down Glen Dun on our way to the sea and Cushenden, as we have seen with its large viaduct. Halfway down the Glen, Chris went down to a local farmhouse to obtain some water from the Antrim hills, for we were very thirsty. At last we came to the viaduct, having camped overnight before we reached the Glen. There was a Catholic church nearby, with the local area being mainly Catholic. We were lucky with the weather for Ireland is a rainy country with many forests – including the forest at Deer Park and the one at Glenarm Castle. At Cushenden there was a small cinema – I forget what we saw but it was quite a busy place. At Cushenden we were greeted by my father and Derek, who was now able to drive us back along the coast road to Ballygally.

With the invention of photography, Ballygally was featured on a number of black-and-white postcards, the headland standing out and the Planter Castle. They feature a time when there was no middle-class settlement in the region. To my recollection there are three black-and-white photos of Ballygally but today they are in colour, shot by John Hinde who has published many picture postcards of Ireland. On one of the postcards it is possible to see the bungalow at Ballygally. Even today Ballygally is a village of the *nouveau riche*, a place now to retire and when I was a teenager a holiday resort for the wealthy during the summer. It was in Ballygally that my brother met Helen Crawford, his future wife, who both now live in retirement in England but make frequent trips back to Northern Ireland.

Chapter Five

When Derek left Queen's University, Belfast, he got a job as a schoolteacher at Sommerdale Secondary School, after which he became a child psychologist based at Belfast on the Antrim Road. He wanted to live in England, so he and Helen left for Manchester where Derek worked for ICI, training managers for the corporation. Helen bought her own car for £400 and got a job selling insurance door-to-door which she did for a number of years, after which she got another job selling commercial wall coverings. In 1969, after travelling from Northern Ireland, they bought a bungalow on a new housing estate in Atherton, near Bolton. For a while after leaving London in 1970 I lived with them, but I wanted a flat of my own.

At Ballygally I used to sometimes buy the *Exchange & Mart* magazine in which was advertised an Adana 8x5 printing machine which cost the sum of about ten pounds. At Ballygally I often felt that I wanted to buy an Adana and sell personal stationery, so I left for England. After working in London, I started by knocking on doors of the new housing estates to obtain orders. I was lucky; on my first day out I obtained three orders during one evening. One hundred sheets of personal stationery cost a guinea, for it was still the age of old money, pounds shillings and pence until decimal arrived in 1971. It was also an age of inflation after the Second World War. On the Adana I printed business cards, invoices and business headings. I also printed some colour work with ink supplied by Adana in Church Street, Twickenham.

When I worked in London I saw an Adana displayed in their shop in Gray's Inn and from that time I was determined to buy one.

At Atherton, my father paid to buy the Adana from the shop which also sold printing paper. The personal stationery that I supplied was printed on Croxley Script measuring seven inches by five inches, rather than Basildon Bond or Queen's Velvet which were quite expensive. At Ballygally I had to say farewell to my mother; from a very early age I was attached to her and she was reluctant for me to work in London. My curiosity about London had started when I was seventeen years of age on our trips to London. From this time I loved walking down Tottenham Court Road to Trafalgar Square When I lived in London, I rented a flat on the Caledonian Road N1. I also liked travelling on the Underground from Tottenham Court Road to the Caledonian Rd. When I was at Trinity College, I saw the Emerald Staff Bureau advertising jobs in London in the *Dublin Evening News*. I would often phone home reporting my progress in the Swinging Sixties.

Chapter Six

I was one of the few people who left Ballygally to work in England. John Harbinson, Derek's friend, left Ballygally to live in Australia. He had qualified as an architect and set up his own practice in Australia. Both Derek and Helen visited John and his wife on a number of occasions, flying out to Australia. When Chris Harbinson left the Portora school he got a job as a journalist on the Larne Times after which he left for Belfast to be a journalist on the *Belfast Telegraph*, a Unionist paper, but I think he was more interested in writing rather than politics. He also worked for the *News Letter* which was the oldest daily in the United Kingdom. Most of his career as a journalist was spent on the *News Letter*.

Before owning his first car he travelled from Larne by rail to Belfast's York Road, from where he walked up York Street to the *Belfast Telegraph* offices at Royal Avenue. In the Larne Times Chris featured articles about Ballygally, what locals were doing and the history of the village. Both Chris and I as teenagers had admired the Planter Castle on the coast road which today has a thriving business with an international reputation.

I always thought that Chris wanted to go to university but alas he did not have enough GCEs Nevertheless, he had a very successful career as a Journalist both on the *Belfast Telegraph* and the *News Letter*. My uncle Jim read the *Belfast Telegraph* which was delivered to Ballygally on the late afternoon bus; he called the paper 'The Halfpenny Liar'. He would send Derek over to the local shop to buy the paper and rang his sailor's bell to hurry Derek up from the shop, for he would stop and talk to his friends. My Uncle Jim would ask Derek to carry his chair into the front room of the bungalow, where my father would read out interesting articles for him after returning from work. As the County Dental Officer for Antrim, he earned the vast sum of £3,000 a year, quite a large amount of money in the fifties. In the sixties my father bought a television that only featured the BBC. I would sit with my mother to *Watch with Mother* which featured the *Flowerpot Men* and *Hank Rides Again*. There was also *Woman's Hour* at two o'clock in the afternoon followed by the news bulletin at six o'clock, but no Northern Ireland news.

When I lived in Manchester I made frequent visits to Ballygally. On several occasions I rode my motorcycle up the A6 to Carlisle, a distance of about one hundred miles and turned west to Dumfries and Galloway to the ferries at Stranraer and over to Larne. The ferries were drive-on and off, the voyage taking about two-and-a-half hours. From Larne I made my way out to the bungalow at Ballygally. After my father's death I stayed with my mother for a few days; sometimes she would write me a cheque for £500 for by now I had an office at 63 Corporation Street in the centre of Manchester, before the Victorian buildings at the end of the street were demolished. My mother was able to continue living in Ballygally for she had her state pension, stocks and shares and my father's pension which he had paid into when he was the County Dental Officer.

My mother died in February 1999, aged 87; she had outlived my father by many years. He died in December 1970 having suffered from depression for most of his life, but it did not interfere with his job at Antrim County Health Committee until the end. He also left a substantial amount of money in his will. She was still able to do her shopping at Ballygally post office, owned by William Collins who was still in business when I visited Ballygally in 1973; he eventually sold the business to a Roman Catholic gentleman, but alas most of Ballygally was mainly Protestant and he went out of business. My mother continued to give the post office her custom.

Ballygally café made lots of money at weekends, selling ice cream and other visitor essentials. The owner, Ronnie Lough, also opened up a small pub in the café buildings along with a restaurant. Lobsters were on the menu; he caught them himself in his boat, leaving out the lobster pots for a good catch. As a teenager I bought my comics at the café then owned by a Mr Kemp, an Englishman. The comics featured western stories and each cost about sixpence. I had quite a good collection. My father also gave me pocket money, two-and-sixpence a week, which I would spend on Mars bars and lots of types of chocolate. Saturday night was also chocolate night and my father would send me over to the café to buy sweets. My father was not a churchgoer but he required me to attend Saint Patrick's Church of Ireland along with my mother. We were given a lift by Mrs Law, who was English.

Chapter Seven

After the death of the Reverend Brown, the new Rector was the Reverend Caldwell, who had been the Chaplin to Holywell Hospital, and who also attended Orange's Academy at night school, for he wanted a degree in Theology at Trinity College Dublin to become an Anglican vicar. Another of my next-door neighbours was Mr and Mrs Green, who made jam. Her nephew and niece – Michael Pinnar and Jacqueline – travelled up from Glenarm where they lived, to visit them. We played tennis on the front lawn which had a metal fence before my father planted trees. Michael Pinnar went on to join the Police Force, as far as I know in London. One of Derek's friends, Kenneth Bell, also joined the police (The Royal Ulster Constabulary) on the eve of the troubles in Northern Ireland.

The Reverend Caldwell was a middle-of-the-road Anglican and his Rectory was situated on the Cairncastle Road in Ballygally. He was anxious to please his congregation at a time when there were movements for reconciliation with the Church of Rome. His chapel lay at the bottom of Cairncastle Road. In the nineteenth century the Church of Ireland, whose see was at Armagh, was the established church and Presbyterians were discriminated against along with the Roman Catholics. Reverend Caldwell may have had an interest in the Ecumenical movement that was taking place with the election of Pope John Paul XXIII to the Papal throne. It was an age when the Roman Catholic Church wanted liberal Popes that would not regard Protestants as heretics. Reverend

Caldwell was no friend of the Pope but he had a lively interest in the doctrine and dogmas of the Roman Catholic Church. Like Reverend Brown, Reverend Caldwell encouraged Sunday School for the young children of Ballygally and Kilwaughter. In Reverend Brown's day, Sandra Bell – about seventeen – presided over the school where conventional Protestantism was taught. I must confess that I did not believe any of the beliefs of Christianity, despite the fact that at Larne Grammar I was given compulsary religious instruction. The same was true of Dungannon Royal, but at Orange's Academy although religious instruction was not compulsory I still attended, having a curiosity about the Church of Rome. The religious instruction given was based on the Church of Rome, which prompted me to buy some books on Protestantism in a shop near Belfast Academical Institution.

When I was at Jaffa College, I met Maurice Barr who worked for the Electricity Board and who wanted to be a Presbyterian Clergyman. Although we were good friends, we argued about the beliefs of the Church of Rome. Maurice was aware that I did not believe in God. My mother, while attending Saint Patrick's Church of Ireland, taught me that it was essential to lead a good life rather than be a stern fan of Christianity. She gave amounts of money to the Church of Ireland each year at Christmas but my father claimed he was a follower of Buddha! Certainly he did not believe in Christianity and when Reverend Caldwell paid us a visit my father made haste to the loft where he had a photographic dark room.

In his sermons Reverend Caldwell dwelled on leading a good life and he did not preach much about the Church of Rome, even though he may have known the local Roman Catholic Priest socially. But the Church of Ireland claimed to be the Catholic Church and that the Roman Catholic Church was in error. Reverend Caldwell encouraged his flock to read the Bible but he was open to the finds of archaeology in connection with his preaching. I first met Mr and Mrs Caldwell when walking along the seafront and I held out my hand to his, explaining that my mother and myself were keen on his sermons. I was about twelve years of age and still at Larne Grammar School, of which Reverend Caldwell was one of the Governors. Saint Patrick's Church of Ireland was quite small, with seating arrangements of about two hundred. It was quite plain inside and very Protestant. It also had stained glass windows and a cross upon the altar, unlike the Roman Catholic Church which was even smaller and served the Roman Catholic farming community. There was a garden party each summer, but this was later discontinued, probably due to lack of attendance. His Rectory was quite large and I visited it on a number of occasions. When I was going into business at 63 Corporation Street, Manchester, I asked Reverend Caldwell to write a character reference for the estate agents I rented the property from the landlords, Watney Mann Brewers. Mr Knox, the solicitor, provided me with a trade reference. At this time I was twenty-three years of age and quite young to be going into business on my own account.

Chapter Eight

In my uncle's day, the drive running up to the bungalow garage was covered in white pebbles from the beach but my father ordered some cement from the Curran Saw Mills and made the drive out of the cement as a do-it-yourself project. The whole process took a number of days and I had cine film of the drive at the bungalow. The garage, which he also built himself, housed his Ford Zodiac. He demolished the original garage and built a new one in which he built his boats, helped by Derek and myself. There was also a small greenhouse that he also built himself and – as we have seen – he also built the larger greenhouse which was the size of a small house. Among his many hobbies at Ballygally was astronomy, and to this effect he built a wooden observatory and made his own mirrors for the telescope, which he also made himself. He was a fan of Patrick Moore the television astronomer and his programme *The Sky at Night*.

The roses he planted in the flowerbeds in the front and back gardens were bought from Macgreedy's and Dixon's on the outskirts of Belfast. He was very green-fingered and I planted some primroses in a flowerbed in the front of the bungalow.

My parents did not attend Sports Day at Larne Grammar where, at the age of eleven, I won a junior cup as the best sportsman of the year, but in the senior school I did not shine.

I had a number of cats; the first one was black which I obtained from Mrs Hunter, a few doors down from the bungalow. My favourite cat was Minksie, an orange-and-white cat which disappeared when my father died. It was very devoted to my father, and my mother quite liked cats too.

I did not like dogs. Sydney Durbridge had an aggressive dog that barked at me and when I made my journeys to the post office; it would try to leap over the wall and attack me. On one occasion it was successful and it bit my bum; Derek and Mr Durbridge restrained the dog and my father called the doctor to give me a tetanus injection.

I was not too keen on the people of Ballygally after being taken away from Riverdale Park Road, but the situation of the bungalow I liked, along with the headland and the views of the coastal headland; Glenarm Head and Fair Head came alive at sunsets. This I would watch from the front room of the bungalow. Even today I regard Ballygally as a bit of a bigoted place: 99% of them Protestants, mainly Presbyterians.

When I was about sixteen, Derek and I ventured over a bit of the Antrim Plateau to Slemish Mountain, that rose about three hundred feet above ground level, Slemish is, of course, associated with Saint Patrick. We climbed to the summit of the mountain. The local farmer accused us of trespassing on his land and when we explained that we were from Ballygally, he was not impressed and said that Ballygally was a place for the rich. Nevertheless, he let us climb Slemish which in the fifth century, the age of Saint Patrick, was inhabited by Lord Miliucc who was Patrick's slave-master. Miliucc was a pagan and Patrick or Succat was a Christian of the Church of Rome.

On other occasions we would play cricket in the large field that lay at the foot of Ballygally Head or Hill. We also played chess of a pocket variety, which Derek nearly always won. We played draughts too and sometimes Monopoly along with my father in the dining room of the bungalow. On another occasion when Derek had bought his Hillman Imp, I accompanied him and his friend James King to Dublin, where we frequented a nightclub on the banks of the River Liffey. We had two or three drinks and this was an age where there were no drink and driving laws in the UK or Eire. Derek bought me a couple of vodka and limes.

James King also went to Larne Grammar and went on to get a degree in Philosophy from Queens University, Belfast.

My father erected a large aerial in the back garden of the bungalow and on clear days, weather permitting, it was possible to receive Scottish television at a time when there was no Ulster Television – even though the BBC had its headquarters at Ormeau Avenue in Belfast and Ulster Television was only a short distance away.

In 1977 when I was living in England and had published my first book on Ulster – *Ulster & Its Future After the Troubles* – I was invited to the BBC to be interviewed by Sean Afferty on *PM Ulster* on Radio Ulster. I was also interviewed by David Duncief of Ulster Television on *UTV Reports* and was featured in the *Belfast Telegraph* by Sandra Chapman. In the book I had predicted the end of the troubles in Northern Ireland.

Visiting my mother for Christmas – she had ordered the turkey, baked plum duff and Christmas cake – I stayed in Ballygally for about a week. I also caught the train to Dublin to place my book in the shops and negotiated some business with the Belfast booksellers. There was high security in the city, for this was the age of the Troubles. I dedicated my book to my mother. From then on, I became determined to promote my books in the media in Manchester. I was frequently on BBC Radio Manchester in Oxford Street. I was also featured six times by Guy Meyler in his court and social column in *The Manchester Evening News*. I am now seventy-six years of age, having written and published thirty-five books on Ireland and other subjects.

I ran *Highfield Press* from the two-up and two-down terraced cottage in Bredbury near Stockport and – as we have seen – it was also the home of my printing business.

I lived in Bredbury for about seven years, during which time I travelled by train from Stockport to Birmingham where for six years I was Ireland political correspondent for BRMB Radio. I did a number of phone-ins and telephone comments on the Troubles in Northern Ireland. I also – on about twelve occasions – had an Irish history spot on *Good Morning Ulster*. I was interviewed on

Liverpool's local BBC radio about my first book. I travelled on the train up to Bradford for the local history programme on Radio Bradford, a commercial station, as was BRMB. I motorbiked over the Brecon Beacons in Wales on my Honda 250 which could do one hundred miles per hour; I was lucky with the weather. I motorbiked to Cardiff and Swansea selling my books. I went along the coast to Swansea and then across to Bristol, home of Harvey's Bristol Cream Sherry. I went to Oxford to Basil Blackwell's bookshop, and from there I travelled north to Birmingham also selling books. At length I reached home and Bredbury from a tour that took about a week.

Eventually I started to sell my books over the phone. At Bredbury I did not have a phone so I sold books by using the Ballygally phone number; Guy Meyler of the *Manchester Evening News* featured a story "If you want to speak to Michael ask his mum" but I did eventually have a telephone.

In 1984 I wanted to live in the country that I wrote about, so I left England to return to Ballygally, my mother… and of course the telephone. I published two of the books in Ballygally, starting in 1990 with *The Twilight Pagans* and *Enemy of England,* the story of Hugh O'Neil's revolt against English rule in the sixteenth century. The rest of the books were published by A H Stockwell Ltd of Bedfordshire. The first book I published with Stockwell was entitled *The Great Siege* and was the story of the siege of Londonderry in 1689. My latest book is now with Stockwell and I expect a proof by mid-September entitled *Ireland 1688 – Wreck of the Spanish Armada.* Although I have published three books on Saint Patrick, I have not however developed any religious faith. If I were to go to church, I would attend the High Church of England whose faith – like Roman Catholicism – was like that of Ireland in the fifth century, the faith of Saint Patrick. In the rock opera *Jesus Christ Superstar* it was said that "Do you think that you are what they say you are?" The world is full of religions claiming to have the monopoly on truth, so which one is right?

Young people today reject the stories in the Bible that feature such acts as raising people from the dead. There is the story of the Creation, which modern believers reject – but neither am I a fan of the Big Bang Theory. Each generation has and will have its beliefs about the Creation, the Catholic Church claiming that God created the heaven and earth in six days and rested on the seventh day and hallowed it.

The bungalow at Ballygally was freehold and my mother did not have to pay ground rent. When she died in 1999, I sold the bungalow and headed for the county town of Antrim that lay near Lough Neagh. I am a fan of county towns, having lived in Chester, a walled county town, for two years. In 1990 I went on holiday to England for a week, travelling via Larne Stranraer and rail to Carlisle where I changed trains to catch the London train that would take me to Manchester Piccadilly.

At Antrim I wrote for the local newspaper, the *Antrim Times* and the *Antrim Guardian*, writing about the local history of the area. I also did some radio work, though not on the English scale. I also visited Ballygally on a few occasions, for its scenery had inspired a lot of my books. I kept in contact with Muriel Harbinson, sending her copies of my books as they were published. Unfortunately, Muriel had a fall recently and sadly died. I have not seen Chris Harbinson for over fifty years and he is probably retired. To the best of my knowledge he lives in Ireland, in Islandmagee near Larne.

When I lived in Ballygally after returning from England, I would make the walk from Ballygally to Carnfunnock country park, which when I was in my teens was open fields. It now has a shop selling books and other tourist memorabilia; there is also a café where I would sometimes have a cup of tea or a Coca-Cola. The distance to Carfunnock was about two miles from Ballygally; there and back it took about an hour. My walk was featured in the *Larne Guardian*; I made it in all weathers with the sea on my left and woodlands on the right. I would also pass through the entrance to Cairndhu Golf Club where Chris and I played golf when he was on holiday from Portora Royal School. Another favourite walk was that up Croft Road from the coast to the Old Mill where there is a scenic bridge under which the river flowed into Ballygally Castle grounds, running onto the sandy beach. There are a number of small cottages on Croft Road and also some larger houses with expensive cars parked in front of the dwellings. From the Old Mill a track runs up to Cairndhu Golf Course and through the grounds of Lady Dixon's former estate. From here the road runs down to the coast road. The golf club is a phenomenon of the early sixties.

***

When I die, I will leave the royalties of my books to my brother Derek and leave instructions to be cremated and buried with my father and mother in the graveyard of Saint Patrick's Church of Ireland, overlooking the North Channel and Ballygally Bay.

Now seventy-six, I live in a private nursing home in Muckamore, County Antrim.

www.ingramcontent.com/pod-product-compliance
Lightning Source LLC
Chambersburg PA
CBHW031531040426
42445CB00009B/488